K-5

MORE
GOOD IDEAS
to Help Young People Develop Good Character

A Supplement to the *Good Ideas* Book, With 42 New
Lessons and Activities for Bringing the
Six Pillars of Character to K-5 Classrooms

By Melissa Mertz
Instructional Designer
Josephson Institute of Ethics

Produced by the Department of Publications
Josephson Institute of Ethics

Wes Hanson
Director of Publications

Steve Nish
Senior Editor

Dan McNeill
Editor

Andrew Acalinovich
Graphics Editor

www.charactercounts.org
www.josephsoninstitute.org

JOSEPH & EDNA
JOSEPHSON
INSTITUTE
OF ETHICS

Published by the Josephson Institute of Ethics
Los Angeles, California

Copyright ©2004 Josephson Institute

All rights reserved under International and Pan-American
Copyright Conventions. Published in the United States by
the Josephson Institute.

www.charactercounts.org / www.josephsoninstitute.org

"CHARACTER COUNTS!", the "Six Pillars of Character," the "Pursuing Victory with Honor" sportsmanship campaign, the "Honor Above All" academic integrity campaign, the "American Youth Character Awards" and
"Character Carousel" are marks of the CHARACTER COUNTS! Coalition, a
project of the Josephson Institute.

ISBN 1-888689-22-6

Manufactured in the United States of America
First Edition

Back Cover Photo of Students on Steps: Keith Gaynes Photography
Printing: Orange Ink, Irvine, CA

– CONTENTS –

Introduction

As communities around the country have rediscovered the critical importance of educating for character, one approach has quickly gained favor — CHARACTER COUNTS!. The reasons are clear: It's flexible, cost-effective and easy to implement. It's nonsectarian and nonpartisan. It's not an add-on or burden for teachers. Study after study shows it works, often dramatically.

And, importantly, its national office is continually developing new programs, services and materials to assist character educators (that is to say, you). A case in point: our *GOOD IDEAS* book grew into a collection of 250 lesson plans, the backbone of our curricular support materials. Now its popularity has inspired two new supplements, one for elementary students and one for teens.

This volume contains 42 fresh activities for grades K-5 (ages 4-11) that highlight the Six Pillars of Character: trustworthiness, respect, responsibility, fairness, caring and citizenship. The foundation of CHARACTER COUNTS!, the Six Pillars are a consistent language that young people readily grasp. As a result, when you integrate these lessons into your curriculum you heighten youngsters' awareness of ethical issues and their responsibilities as individuals of character.

We hope you find these activities useful. Even if you teach only one age group, please peruse the entire book. An idea presented for, say, first graders may be adaptable to fifth graders with only minor changes. In addition, we have placed icons beside lessons particularly relevant to three of the issues educators find most pressing today: bullying, cheating and diversity. (You may also like to know that we now offer "Honor Above All," a suite of resources to help you promote academic integrity and prevent cheating, geared mainly toward middle and high school students.)

We are interested in hearing feedback about your experience with these lessons, as well as what else you are doing with CHARACTER COUNTS! in your classroom and community. Please send your news and ideas to ccnews@jiethics.org. Thank you for all your efforts to educate for character and build a better world.

THE SIX PILLARS OF CHARACTER

TRUSTWORTHINESS

- Be honest.
- Don't deceive, cheat or steal.
- Be reliable — do what you say you'll do.
- Have the courage to do the right thing.
- Build a good reputation.
- Be loyal — stand by your family, friends and country.

RESPECT

- Treat others with respect; follow the Golden Rule.
- Be tolerant of differences.
- Use good manners, not bad language.
- Be considerate of the feelings of others.
- Don't threaten, hit or hurt anyone.
- Deal peacefully with anger, insults and disagreements.

RESPONSIBILITY

- Do what you are supposed to do.
- Persevere: keep on trying!
- Always do your best.
- Use self-control.
- Be self-disciplined.
- Think before you act — consider the consequences.
- Be accountable for your choices.

FAIRNESS

- Play by the rules.
- Take turns and share.
- Be open-minded; listen to others.
- Don't take advantage of others.
- Don't blame others carelessly.

CARING

- Be kind.
- Be compassionate; show you care.
- Express gratitude.
- Forgive others.
- Help people in need.

CITIZENSHIP

- Do your share to make your school and community better.
- Cooperate.
- Stay informed; vote.
- Be a good neighbor.
- Obey laws and rules.
- Respect authority.
- Protect the environment

GOOD IDEAS

to Help 4- to 6-Year-Olds Develop Good Character

IDEA #1

Trust Throughout the Day

OVERVIEW: Students discuss how trust plays a role in their lives all day, every day, and draw a picture of a world with trust and a world without it.

PREPARATION / MATERIALS:
- blank white paper, one sheet for each student
- crayons or markers

PROCEDURE:

Ask students, *What do you think it means to trust someone?* Prompt them to think of all the times they trust someone in a typical day. For example, they trust that:

- Their parents will wake them on time in the morning.
- No one will run a red light on the way to school.
- The teacher will tell them correct facts.
- Their friends will play games by the rules.
- No one will take the papers from their desk when they go to the bathroom.
- The cook in a restaurant will prepare food cleanly.

Then ask children to notice how many ways other people trust them. For example:

- Their parents trust them to eat the lunch they packed, or buy nutritious food at the cafeteria.
- Their parents trust them to clean their rooms if told.
- Their teacher trusts them to return art supplies in good condition.
- Their teacher trusts them to deliver a message to the office without goofing around on the way.
- Their friends trust them to keep secrets.

Next, say, *Imagine what life would be like if you couldn't trust people.* Walk them through a typical day, as before, this time asking, *What if you couldn't trust them to do what they are supposed to?* Have students draw a picture of a world where everyone is trustworthy, and next to that, draw a picture of a world where no one is trustworthy. Display the artwork on a bulletin board entitled, "Trust Means the World to Us."

When somebody lies, somebody loses.

— **Stephanie Ericsson**
American writer
(b. 1953)

IDEA #2

Chopping Down Lies

OVERVIEW: Students learn the tale of George Washington chopping down the cherry tree and telling the truth about it. Although the story is probably fiction, its moral about candor is valuable nonetheless. Students then make construction paper axes that will remind them to "chop down" or "cut out" lies from their daily lives.

PREPARATION / MATERIALS:
- story of "George and the Cherry Tree" (provided)
- stapler
- piece of brown construction paper (to be rolled for ax handle), one for each student
- photocopy of ax head on gray paper (or outline of ax head on gray construction paper), one for each student
- pair of scissors, one for each student
- transparent tape, three pieces for each student

A man who

doesn't trust

himself can never

really trust

anyone else.

— Cardinal De Retz
French Cardinal
and politician
(1614-1679)

PROCEDURE:

Before the lesson, gather all the materials necessary for each student to make an "honesty ax" for George Washington. Either photocopy the ax head onto gray paper, or draw the outline of the ax head onto sheets of gray construction paper.

Read students the story about George Washington's famous encounter with the cherry tree, and his decision to tell the truth about it. Make sure children understand that the tale itself is not necessarily true, but is rather a legend that has come down to us about our first president as a youngster.

After reading the story, discuss it. Ask:

- Why do you think Washington told the truth even though he knew he could get in trouble?
- Have you ever told the truth about something you did, though you knew it could lead to punishment? Why did you tell the truth?
- Why is it especially important for our president to be honest?

Give each student one uncut ax head, one sheet of brown construction paper, a pair of safety scissors and three pieces of transparent tape. Have students roll up the brown construction paper to make the handle, then tape it. Next, have them cut out the ax head from the gray paper and wrap the middle around one end of the brown handle. Pass around a stapler and have students staple the ax head to the handle, and at the "sharp" edge. Have students write their names on the ax head.

Tell students, *Close your eyes and remember a time when you told a lie. Now imagine that the lie is a tree. This tree is sick because it represents a lie. It needs to be chopped down. Take your ax and chop it down.* Students can pretend to chop down the lie. Tell students, *Next time you feel like you want to lie, think of your honesty ax and chop down the lie before you say it.* Keep the axes on display to remind each student to cut out lies and lead lives based on trustworthiness.

Adapted from an idea found on http://www.kinderteacher.com/GeorgeWashingtonIdeas.htm.

George Washington and the Cherry Tree

When George was about six years old, he was made the wealthy master of a hatchet of which, like most little boys, he was extremely fond. He went about chopping everything that came his way.

One day, as he wandered about the garden amusing himself by hacking his mother's pea-sticks, he found a beautiful, young English cherry tree, of which his father was most proud. He tried the edge of his hatchet on the trunk of the tree and barked it so that it died.

Some time after this, his father discovered what had happened to his favorite tree. He came into the house in great anger, and demanded to know who the mischievous person was who had cut away the bark. Nobody could tell him anything about it.

Just then George, with his little hatchet, came into the room.

"George," said his father, "do you know who has killed my beautiful little cherry tree yonder in the garden? I would not have taken five guineas for it!"

This was a hard question to answer, and for a moment George was staggered by it, but quickly recovering himself he cried:

"I cannot tell a lie, father, you know I cannot tell a lie! I did cut it with my little hatchet."

The anger died out of his father's face, and taking the boy tenderly in his arms, he said:

"My son, that you should not be afraid to tell the truth is more to me than a thousand trees! Yes, though they were blossomed with silver and had leaves of the purest gold!"

By M.L. Weems, from *Good Stories for Great Holidays,* edited by Frances Jenkins Olcott, Boston: Houghton Mifflin Company, 1914. (This book has passed into the public domain and therefore its contents are reproducible without permission.)

● read up and reach out at www.charactercounts.org ●

More Good Ideas to Help Young People Develop Good Character

IDEA #3

Teasing and Bullying: *Say Something*

> **OVERVIEW:** After being read the book *Say Something*, students talk about teasing and the importance of standing up for others.
>
> **PREPARATION / MATERIALS:**
> * copy of *Say Something* by Peggy Moss

PROCEDURE:

A free society is a place where it's safe to be unpopular.

— **Adlai Stevenson**
U.S. politician, author
(1900-1965)

Bullying is a major problem in schools today, yet a very small minority of children are actually bullies. Many more are victims. But the majority are silent bystanders. The book *Say Something* addresses that silent majority and encourages these students to take action.

Read the book to your class. Then conduct a discussion about bullying. Stress that you are not asking students to "name names" right now, but rather you just want to talk about the overall issue. Suggested questions include:

* Does bullying happen at our school?
* Have you ever been bullied?
* How did it feel?
* Have you ever seen someone else get teased or bullied?
* Did you do anything? Why or why not?
* If you were being bullied or teased, would you want someone else to stand up for you?
* What are some ways you can help someone who is often bullied or teased?

Emphasize that you do not want students to get in the middle of fights or put themselves in dangerous situations. Instead, you want to encourage them to expand their circle of friends, to be friendly with students whom they have ignored. And when they do see teasing or bullying, they shouldn't stand idly by and watch, but rather should tell an adult. Later, they should approach the victim and get to know him or her. Tell students: *Respect is about treating others the way you want to be treated. If you were being picked on, you would want someone to help you.*

Say Something *is published by Tilbury House Publishers, ©2004.*

IDEA #4

Multilingual Respect

OVERVIEW: Children make mini-posters with the word *respect* in different languages and decorate them with pictures of children from around the world.

PREPARATION / MATERIALS:
- copy of "Respect in Many Languages Handout," one for each student (or copy onto an overhead transparency)
- blank paper, one sheet for each student
- crayons or markers
- magazines to cut up (optional)
- scissors (optional)
- glue (optional)

PROCEDURE:

Chances are, in any given classroom there are some children who speak a language besides English. Take a survey and write down on the board any languages your students speak. Ask if their parents speak any others that the children do not. Have students who know another language say the word *respect* in that language. If possible, have them come up to the board and write the word in the foreign language.

If English is the only language in your classroom or you want to enrich your class's list, copy and hand out the following page, which lists *respect* in many different languages.

Once you have presented a list of *respect* in various languages, tell students: *Even though every language has a different word for respect, it means the same thing around the world.* Emphasize that no matter what language someone speaks, or what country they come from, they deserve respect. Ask students to name ways to show respect.

Arrange students into groups of three or four and assign each group *respect* in a different language. Distribute blank paper, coloring implements, and if possible, magazines, scissors and glue.

Have students copy the foreign-language *respect* onto their paper in a decorative fashion. Around it students can either draw pictures of students from all over the world, or glue magazine photos of children from varied ethnic backgrounds. Display the finished products on a bulletin board entitled "Respect Around the World."

*V*ariety's the

very spice of life.

— William Cowper
English poet
(1731-1800)

Respect in Many Languages

Spanish: respeto

French: respect

German: respekt

Italian: rispetto

Chinese: 尊敬

Dutch: eerbied

Arabic: إحترام (ihitiram)

Greek: σεβασμός (sevasmos)

Portuguese: respeito

Russian: уважение

Afrikaans: aansien

Tagalog: galang

Swahili: ustahivu

Turkish: saygi

Japanese: 尊敬 (sonkei)

IDEA #5

Class Pet

OVERVIEW: Groups of students take responsibility for the care of a caged pet in the classroom.

PREPARATION / MATERIALS:
- pet care schedule (template provided)
- small animal, such as a mouse, hamster, gerbil or fish
- cage or aquarium
- animal food
- containers for food and water
- litter

Distance tests a horse's strength; time reveals a man's character.

— Chinese proverb

PROCEDURE:

A class pet gives students the chance to show responsibility on a daily basis. Tell them that they will be adopting an animal. You can either decide what kind of animal ahead of time or let students vote on it.

To emphasize that responsibility starts before the pet has even arrived, have students list all the items they will need to take care of the animal, and all the tasks they will have to carry out. Purchase the animal and supplies at a local pet store. If funds are tight, consider raising money with a bake sale or similar event. In fact, students will appreciate the animal more if they earn it.

The first week, model for students how to check the food and water, clean the litter, and otherwise care for the pet. Then assign groups of three to four students to take responsibility for the animal each following week. Keep track of whose turn it is on the schedule (provided). You can break the responsibility down into smaller jobs, if you prefer, such as check/refill food, empty/refill water, and clean litter. Assign a second group to be a monitor, to assure that the first group is doing well and to act as backup in case a student is absent. Each Monday the experienced group should guide the new group, showing them what to do.

At the end of every week, meet briefly with the group that cared for the pet that week. Ask, *Did everyone do their job when and how they were supposed to? How did you feel about taking care of the animal? Did you look forward to it? Is the responsibility of caring for a pet worth the pleasure of its company?*

Pet Care Schedule

Day/Date	Names of Students	Job

IDEA #6

Taking On New Responsibilities

OVERVIEW: Students take on a new responsibility at home and discuss the positive and negative results.

PREPARATION / MATERIALS:
- copy of letter to parents, one for each student

PROCEDURE:

Most 4- to 6-year-olds will have few responsibilities at home. This activity gives them a chance to try taking one on, to see if they're ready.

Tell students, *Think of one thing your parents still do for you at home, that you could probably do for yourself.* Possibilities include tying children's shoes, making their bed, picking out their clothes, putting away their toys, and making their lunch.

Hand out the letter to parents asking them to let their children do this task for themselves during the next week. Have students write out the responsibility in the space provided, and sign the bottom of the letter.

After students have performed the new task for one day, hold a brief class discussion to give them encouragement. Ask, *How is the new responsibility going? Were you able to finish it all by yourself? What was hard? What was easy?*

At the end of the week, ask students to talk about how the new job went. Ask, *Is your new responsibility more or less difficult than you expected? How do you feel after finishing it all on your own? Why is it important for you to do things for yourself instead of always getting help from your parents? How many of you will keep this new responsibility next week?*

Adapted from a lesson submitted by Alex Reardon, coordinator of character education at Highland Renaissance Academy.

N o bird soars

too high if he soars

with his own wings.

— William Blake
English poet and artist (1757-1827)

Date _____

Dear Mom and Dad,

Right now in school we are learning about the character trait of responsibility. I am learning that I am responsible for my own actions and behavior. I would like to practice being responsible this week by taking on a new task by myself.

The task I would like to take on is:

_____

_____

_____

At the end of the week, I will tell my classmates about the experience of doing this task on my own.

I appreciate you helping me to become a responsible person.

Love,

_____

IDEA #7

The Speaker Has the Floor

OVERVIEW: Students use a tangible object to show who "has the floor" during discussions.

PREPARATION / MATERIALS:
- walking stick or fun hat

PROCEDURE:

Two aspects of fairness are taking turns and listening to others. To help students see more easily whose turn it is to speak during discussions or other activities, have a walking stick or a fun hat that gets passed around. Whoever has that item "has the floor" and no one else can interrupt. When the speaker finishes, he or she passes the item to the next speaker.

When introducing this concept to students, discuss the meaning of fairness. Possible discussion questions are:

1. What does being fair mean to you?
2. Describe a time when someone was unfair to you. What did you do about it?
3. Does being fair mean everything is equal? For example, would it be fair for an older brother in high school to have the same bedtime as you? (Use this example to explain why the teacher can take the talking stick at any time and claim the floor.)
4. Why is it fair only if everyone gets to share their opinion and say what they want to say?
5. Why is it important to take turns?

Courage is what it takes to stand up and speak; courage is also what it takes to sit down and listen.

— Carl Hermann Voss
Author and scholar of religion

IDEA #8

Fair or Unfair?

> **OVERVIEW:** To reinforce the concept of fairness, students decide whether a situation is fair or unfair and stand on one side of the room to indicate their opinion.
>
> **PREPARATION / MATERIALS:**
> none

A person of character takes as much trouble to discover what is right as lesser men take to discover what will pay.

— Confucius
Chinese philosopher
(551-479 B.C.)

PROCEDURE:

Tell students, *Today we are going to play a game called Fair or Unfair? I will read a sentence and you have to decide if it describes something that is fair or unfair. Everyone who thinks it is fair will stand over here* [point to one side of the room] *and everyone who thinks it is unfair will stand over here* [point to the other side].

Read the following statements and have students move to one side of the room or the other. If any statement divides the class almost evenly, you have an opportunity to discuss opposing points of view.

- Everyone takes turns working on the classroom computer.
- Your brother takes all of the cookies on the plate.
- Your mom says you can't watch TV tonight because you didn't clean your room.
- Your dog sleeps outside while you sleep inside.
- Your older sister gets an allowance but you don't.
- Your older brother has a bedtime that is two hours later than yours.
- Your parents are allowed to drive but you aren't.
- You have 20 minutes of homework, but high schoolers have two hours of homework.
- Your teacher says everyone has to stay after class because one student misbehaved.
- Your friend gets 10 minutes on the swing and you get five minutes.
- You aren't invited to your classmate's birthday party.
- Your newborn baby sister gets more attention than you.

IDEA #9

Character Cameras

OVERVIEW: Students compliment each other by writing adjectives on "character cameras," paper cutouts shaped like cameras.

PREPARATION / MATERIALS:
- copy of word list, one for each student
- camera pattern photocopied on blue and yellow paper (one blue and one yellow per student)
- scissors
- CD player and any upbeat CD
- blank paper, one sheet for each student
- crayons or markers
- glue

PROCEDURE:

Distribute the word list and discuss the meaning of each word with students. (You can incorporate a lesson on antonyms and synonyms here if you like.) Have students write their names on their lists and circle five words they think describe themselves.

Ask students, *How many of you have taken a picture with a camera?* Show them a real camera if possible. Say, *Today you will pretend that you have a special kind of camera, one that doesn't take snapshots of people's faces, but rather snapshots of people's character.* Explain character, if you haven't already.

Hand out scissors and the camera patterns, one blue and one yellow per student. Have students cut them out and write their names on the bottom of each camera. Then each student creates a "self-portrait" by writing the five words they chose from the list on the blue camera and leaving it on his or her desk.

Students then take their yellow camera, word list, and crayon and sit in a circle on the floor. As the music begins, they pass their yellow cameras to the right, and continue passing them until the music stops. Then they choose a word from the list that best describes the student whose camera they now have. Repeat this procedure until each camera has five words. Tell students not to duplicate words already written on the camera, and to choose only from words on the list. If a student gets his own camera when the music stops, he should trade with someone nearby.

*W*e worry about what a child will be tomorrow, yet we forget that he is someone today.

— attributed to Stacia Tauscher

Have students give the cameras back to their owners and return to their seats. Distribute blank sheets of paper and glue. Students should glue their cameras next to each other on the paper for easy comparison.

If you wish, display the cameras on a bulletin board to remind students of the compliments they gave and received.

Inspired by an activity posted by Lisa Schmidli on http://www.successlink.org/great3/ g2313.htm.

Word List

Athletic	Kind
Brave	Loving
Calm	Loyal
Caring	Neat
Cheerful	Nice
Confident	Patient
Considerate	Polite
Cool	Positive
Courteous	Sensitive
Friendly	Serious
Fun	Silly
Funny	Smart
Generous	Strong
Happy	Studious
Helpful	Thoughtful
Honest	Unselfish

● read up and reach out at www.charactercounts.org ●

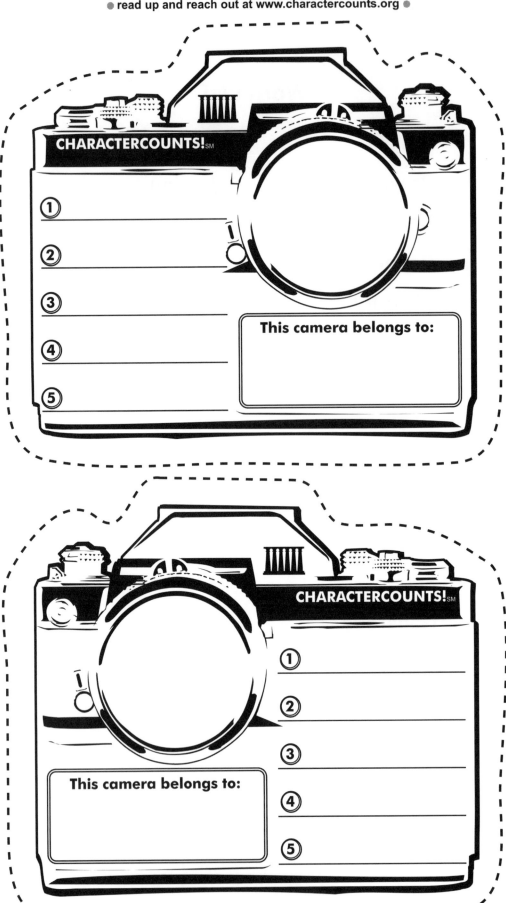

CHARACTERCOUNTS!sm

① _____
② _____
③ _____
④ _____
⑤ _____

This camera belongs to:

CHARACTERCOUNTS!sm

① _____
② _____
③ _____
④ _____
⑤ _____

This camera belongs to:

IDEA #10

Get-Well Cards

OVERVIEW: Students make get-well cards for classmates who miss more than one day of school due to illness or injury.

PREPARATION / MATERIALS:
- construction paper in assorted colors
- crayons or markers
- other decorative items, like glitter or ribbons (optional)

The deepest principle in human nature is the craving to be appreciated.

— William James
American philosopher and psychologist
(1842-1910)

PROCEDURE:

When students miss school due to illness or injury, they sometimes feel left out. Knowing that the teacher and students are thinking of them will cheer them up, and reaching out to the absent students will teach classmates about compassion.

At the beginning of the year, decide your cutoff period for students to qualify for a card. If absences are common, you may want to send a card only if a student misses more than, say, three days of school.

Have students make either one giant card or smaller individual cards wishing the absent student a speedy recovery. On the board, write an example of what to say inside the card:

Dear _____,

I hope you get well soon. We miss you at school.

Sincerely,

_____

If possible, deliver the card(s) to the ill student at home or have the student's parent pick it up with the make-up work.

Alternately, students can design a welcome-back card to give the absent student on his or her return.

IDEA #11

Recycling Drive

> **OVERVIEW:** Students learn which items they can recycle, then collect them and take (or send) them to a recycling center or plant, donating the proceeds to an environmental charity.
>
> **PREPARATION / MATERIALS:**
> - examples of recyclable materials, such as an empty plastic bottle, empty soda can, newspaper, and cereal box
> - copy of letter to parents, one for each student

Again and again, the impossible problem is solved when we see that the problem is only a tough decision waiting to be made.

— Robert H. Schuller
American minister and author
(b. 1926)

PROCEDURE:

A good citizen takes care of the environment. One easy way students can help is to recycle. Show students examples of items they can recycle (for a concise list, visit http://www.obviously.com/recycle/guides/shortest.html) and explain that when they recycle something, it gets melted down (glass, plastic, aluminum) or turned into pulp (paper, cardboard) and then made into new objects. As an example, hold up a newspaper. Tell students, *If you throw this paper in the trash, it will just take up space in our landfills, and never be useful again. But if you recycle it, it will reappear as a new newspaper in a few weeks or months. That's why all citizens must do their part to produce less trash.*

Tell students they will participate in a big project to increase recycling. Get other classes involved, if possible. Decide which recyclable item the class would like to focus on, such as plastic bottles, aluminum cans or newspapers. (Glass bottles are a bad idea, for safety reasons.) Then send a letter home to parents explaining the project. A sample is provided on the next page.

Have students save the items and bring them to school once a week for a month. Then take all the recyclables to a local recycling center (and if a recycling plant is nearby, arrange a field trip). Donate the proceeds to an environmental charity such as the Sierra Club, Conservation Fund, National Park Foundation or Nature Conservancy. (For a list of worthy charities, visit http://www.charitywatch.org/toprated.html#enviro).

Suggestion: Organize the recycling drive around Earth Day, which takes place each year on April 22.

Letter to Parents
About Recycling Drive

Dear Parents,

As you may know, Earth Day is approaching. To teach your children the importance of recycling and how it can help the environment, we are organizing a recycling drive.

We will collect plastic bottles. Please have your children <u>rinse out</u> and set aside all plastic bottles that would otherwise go in the trash. Below is the collection schedule. On each day listed, have your children bring in all their bottles in tied plastic garbage bags (which will be reused or recycled).

Collection Days

_____

_____

_____

_____

_____

We will take all the bottles to a recycling center, and donate the proceeds to _____.

If you have any questions or concerns about this project, please contact me at _____. As always, thank you for your help.

Sincerely,

_____

IDEA #12

Silent Cooperation

OVERVIEW: Without communicating verbally, students form a line according to preassigned numbers.

PREPARATION / MATERIALS:
- slips of paper numbered sequentially, one for each student

The most important thing in any relationship is not what you get but what you give.... In any case, the giving of love is an education in itself.

— Eleanor Roosevelt
American First Lady and social activist (1884-1962)

PROCEDURE:
Cooperation is key to good citizenship. Working together, people can accomplish much more than they can working individually.

Tell students, *You are going to play a game to practice your cooperation skills. I am going to give you a slip of paper with a number on it. Do not say the number out loud or tell anyone your number.* [Hand out the numbered slips of paper in a random order.] *Memorize the number on your paper. Now write your name on your numbered paper.* Then go around the room and collect the papers. Keep these so you can check the students' organization later. Tell students, *Starting now, there is to be no talking at all. I would like you to line up single file in order of your numbers, lowest to highest. You can communicate, but <u>not by talking</u>. Be creative. The only rule is that there must be silence while you complete this activity. There is no time limit. If you forget your number, see me and I will remind you.*

This activity will likely begin with some confusion but if you keep reminding students to silently cooperate with each other, it should work out. At least one student will start using nonverbal communication, such as hand gestures and facial expressions, and others will catch on.

Once students appear to have finished the task, tell them they may talk but not change places. Go through the line and have each student say his or her number. Double check with the slips of paper. No more than one or two students should be out of order.

Ask students, *Do you think this exercise was easy or hard? What made cooperating more difficult than usual? How were you able to solve that problem? Did anyone get frustrated and refuse to cooperate? How did that make the task even more difficult?*

Extension: If students enjoyed this game, they can try a more complex version: organizing themselves by birth date.

IDEA #13

Character Currency

OVERVIEW: Students earn "funny money" called Character Currency for displaying strong character. They can redeem this for small rewards such as leaving early for recess.

PREPARATION / MATERIALS:
- photocopied sheets of Character Currency, cut into individual bills

PROCEDURE:

The true rewards of character are qualities like a sense of well-being and a clear conscience. However, at a very early age, tangible rewards can provide strong motivation for students to get into the habit of displaying good character.

Tell students, *Another word for money is currency, and you are going to have the chance to earn Character Currency. This is fake money that I will hand out when I see you displaying good character. You will be able to use this "funny money" to buy special privileges.* List the privileges, which may include:

- one extra minute at recess
- choosing their seat for the day
- going first for show and tell
- being the line leader
- getting to use the good markers

Tell students you will look for acts that demonstrate one or more of the Six Pillars, such as:

- helping a classmate
- helping the teacher
- cleaning up without being told
- turning in all assignments for a day (or a week)
- complimenting a classmate

Make sure you explain to students that Character Currency is not real money and won't buy them things in real life. Also make it clear that you created this money for fun to use in the classroom, but copying real money is illegal. Make a game out of finding all the things that are different between a real dollar bill and Character Currency.

You must be fit

to give before you

can be fit

to receive.

— James Stephens
Irish novelist and poet
(1882-1950)

read up and reach out at www.charactercounts.org

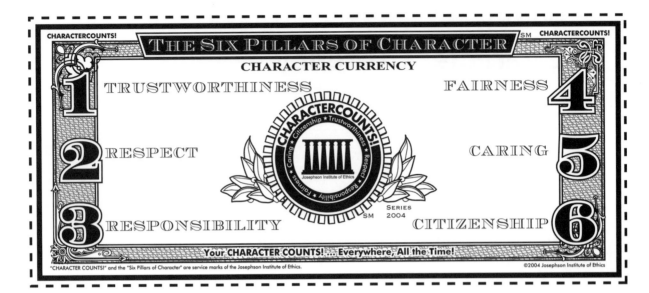

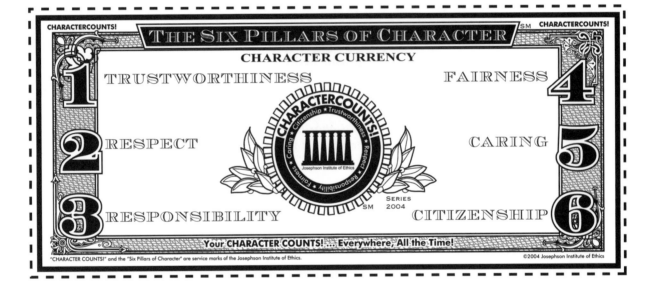

IDEA #14

Character Carousel Puppets

OVERVIEW: Students make finger puppets based on the six animals in the Character Carousel, then create and perform a skit about showing good character, using the puppets.

PREPARATION / MATERIALS:
- copy of Character Carousel finger puppets sheet, one for each student or group of students
- crayons or markers
- scissors
- transparent tape
- set of pre-made puppets (optional)

PROCEDURE:

If students are not familiar with the Character Carousel animals, introduce them. Tell them that each of the Six Pillars of Character has an animal to represent it. Trustworthiness is a camel, Respect is a lion, Responsibility is an elephant, Fairness is a giraffe, Caring is a kangaroo, and Citizenship is a bear. Read the more detailed descriptions from the information sheet on the next page, and show students images of the animals.

Decide in advance whether each student will make one puppet or a whole set, working alone or in a group. Also decide whether you will have a set of puppets pre-made as examples.

Tell students, *You are going to make finger puppets of these six animals, and then you will make up a puppet show about having good character.* Show students the pre-made samples of the puppets, if you have them. Distribute materials accordingly, have students color and cut out the puppets, then help students put together the puppets by wrapping the paper strips around their fingers and taping.

Once they finish the puppets, tell students to think about everything they have learned about the Six Pillars. You may wish to remind them of other activities they have done. Have them create a brief (under five minutes) skit in which the characters either demonstrate good character or learn a lesson about it. If you would like to provide more structure for the skit, say, *The animals of the Character Carousel have just heard that a new student will be joining the class. What advice will each animal give to the new student?* Have students perform their puppet shows for the rest of the class.

Inspired by an activity in What's a Parent to Do? *by Peggy Adkins, a publication of* **CHARACTER COUNTS!** *and the Josephson Institute.*

*F**or many children, joy comes as the result of mining something unique and wondrous about themselves from some inner shaft.*

— Thomas J. Cottle
American professor of education

The Character Carousel

The Character Carousel is a group of six animals designed to help young children learn about the "Six Pillars of Character." The Carousel animals are featured in a puppet-making activity on the following pages.

Shinrai (derived from the Japanese for "trust") is the CAMEL who always keeps her promises, always does what she says she'll do and is loyal, honest and punctual.

Austus (derived from the Estonian for "respect") is the LION who is confident that respect is one of the highest qualities one can have — for nature, for others and for oneself.

Ansvar (derived from the Norwegian for "responsible") is the ELEPHANT with colorful ribbons tied around his trunk and tail to help him remember his responsibilities.

Guisto (derived from the Italian for "fair") is the GIRAFFE who always tries to do what's right. Guisto uses his long neck to see all sides of any issue and has a gentle way of helping others do the same.

Karina (derived from the Spanish for "caring") is the KANGAROO who has a seemingly endless supply of "things" inside her pouch, including a special box of little hearts for children she meets on her travels.

Kupa (derived from the Hawaiian for "citizen") is the BEAR who considers herself a citizen of the world. A philosopher and poet, she believes that we are all part of the same family and must do our share to help each other.

● read up and reach out at www.charactercounts.org ●

Character Carousel Finger Puppets

THE SIX PILLARS OF CHARACTER

TRUSTWORTHINESS

- Be honest.
- Don't deceive, cheat or steal.
- Be reliable — do what you say you'll do.
- Have the courage to do the right thing.
- Build a good reputation.
- Be loyal — stand by your family, friends and country.

RESPECT

- Treat others with respect; follow the Golden Rule.
- Be tolerant of differences.
- Use good manners, not bad language.
- Be considerate of the feelings of others.
- Don't threaten, hit or hurt anyone.
- Deal peacefully with anger, insults and disagreements.

RESPONSIBILITY

- Do what you are supposed to do.
- Persevere: keep on trying!
- Always do your best.
- Use self-control.
- Be self-disciplined.
- Think before you act — consider the consequences.
- Be accountable for your choices.

FAIRNESS

- Play by the rules.
- Take turns and share.
- Be open-minded; listen to others.
- Don't take advantage of others.
- Don't blame others carelessly.

CARING

- Be kind.
- Be compassionate; show you care.
- Express gratitude.
- Forgive others.
- Help people in need.

CITIZENSHIP

- Do your share to make your school and community better.
- Cooperate.
- Stay informed; vote.
- Be a good neighbor.
- Obey laws and rules.
- Respect authority.
- Protect the environment

GOOD IDEAS

to Help <u>6- to 9-Year-Olds</u> Develop Good Character

IDEA #15

Building Trustworthiness

OVERVIEW: For one week, students use a top-10 list to keep track of how they are building trustworthiness in their character each day. Parents sign off on the checklist and students earn certificates.

PREPARATION/MATERIALS:
- copy of trustworthiness chart, one for each student
- copy of trustworthiness certificate, one for every student who has earned one

PROCEDURE:

There are many ways to demonstrate trustworthiness. Making a top-10 list of these ways can be fun and useful. Conduct a brainstorming session and have students suggest ways they can become more trustworthy, such as keep promises, tell the truth, do what you're told, be loyal, admit when you're wrong, never cheat, etc. Write students' ideas on the board. Then have the class come to a consensus on the ten best ways to build trustworthiness.

Next, hand out photocopies of the chart on the next page. Tell students to fill in the ten spaces on the top according to the list they just developed. Then say to students, *You are going to analyze your own lives every day for a week and write down everything you do to become more trustworthy. At the end of the week, have your mom or dad sign off on the chart.* Recognize students' efforts by awarding them a trustworthiness certificate (see page 37), which will also serve as a reminder to continue the journey toward trustworthiness.

Note: If you are interested in establishing a more comprehensive character recognition program, **CHARACTER COUNTS!** offers an implementation kit to aid you in presenting official American Youth Character Awards. Providing you with instructions, nomination forms, judging forms, certificates, sample fliers, a press release, and sheet music with a CD for the ceremony, the kit makes it easy to honor both youths who exhibit exemplary character, as well as the adults who influence them. Visit http://www.charactercounts.org/ayca/details.htm for more information.

Show me a man who cannot bother to do little things and I'll show you a man who cannot be trusted to do big things.

— Lawrence D. Bell
American aircraft manufacturer
(1894-1956)

Inspired by a lesson plan from Lieutenant Grant Pierre of the St. John Parish Police Department, posted at http://www.nasro.org/members/lessons/buildingtrustworthiness.doc.

Ways to Build Trustworthiness

1.	6.
2.	7.
3.	8.
4.	9.
5.	10.

How I Am Building Trustworthiness

MON

_____

_____

TUE

_____

_____

WED

_____

_____

THU

_____

_____

FRI

_____

_____

SAT

_____

_____

SUN

_____

_____

_____   _____
Student Name   Parent Signature

TRUSTWORTHINESS

A person who is trustworthy ...
- Is honest in their words and actions.
- Keeps their promises.
- Stands up for their beliefs and does what it right.
- Is a good friend.

This certificate honors your commitment to being a trustworthy person.

_____   _____
signed by   date

THE SIX PILLARS OF CHARACTER
TRUSTWORTHINESS · RESPECT · RESPONSIBILITY · FAIRNESS · CARING · CITIZENSHIP
"CHARACTER COUNTS!" and the "Six Pillars of Character" are service marks of the Josephson Institute of Ethics.

TRUSTWORTHINESS

A person who is trustworthy ...
- Is honest in their words and actions.
- Keeps their promises.
- Stands up for their beliefs and does what it right.
- Is a good friend.

This certificate honors your commitment to being a trustworthy person.

_____   _____
signed by   date

THE SIX PILLARS OF CHARACTER
TRUSTWORTHINESS · RESPECT · RESPONSIBILITY · FAIRNESS · CARING · CITIZENSHIP
"CHARACTER COUNTS!" and the "Six Pillars of Character" are service marks of the Josephson Institute of Ethics.

● read up and reach out at www.charactercounts.org ●

IDEA #16

The Sultan and the Seeds

HONOR
ABOVE ALL SM
anti-cheating

OVERVIEW: Students read (or listen to) a folk tale about honesty and discuss the importance of integrity.

PREPARATION / MATERIALS:
- copy of "The Sultan and the Seeds" for each student, unless you choose to read it to them

---

*R*ather fail with

honor than succeed

by fraud.

— Sophocles
Greek dramatist
(496-406 B.C.)

PROCEDURE:

Read students the story of "The Sultan and the Seeds" on the next page, or distribute copies for students to read themselves. Then conduct a discussion about honesty and integrity. Among the questions you might ask:

- Why did the sultan give dead seeds to his sons in the first place?
- Why do you think the other eight sons replaced the seeds that wouldn't grow with new, healthy seeds?
- How do you think the other eight sons felt when they found out their father knew they'd switched seeds?
- How do you think the father felt when he saw eight of his sons bringing flourishing plants?
- Do you think the sultan was dishonest in giving this task to his sons? Why or why not?
- Pal earned a huge reward, but often in life the only reward for honesty is the satisfaction of your own integrity. What do you think Pal would have done if he had not been made the new sultan?
- The sultan chose Pal as his successor because of Pal's honor. Why does a leader need to be honorable?
- The nine brothers all thought their father was testing their plant-growing skills, but he was really testing their honor. Would you pass an honor test? Why or why not?

Michael Josephson, founder of the Josephson Institute and **CHARACTER COUNTS!,** *has told this story in his daily radio commentary.*

The Sultan and the Seeds

An old sultan prided himself on having established a kingdom that was just, and he wanted his successor to continue that legacy. So he gathered his nine sons and gave each one a single seed, saying, "I want each of you to plant and nurture your seed. In one year I will judge the results of your efforts and choose the next sultan."

Within months the sons were bragging about how well their seeds had grown—all but Pal, who was unable to produce any growth at all. After a year, the sultan examined each pot and was amazed at the array of beautiful plants. When he came to Pal's lifeless pot he asked what happened. Pal replied humbly, "As hard as I tried, my seed did not grow. I think I was chosen to serve rather than lead."

"My son," the sultan said, "you *have* been chosen to serve, and you shall do so by leading this kingdom as its next sultan. You alone among your brothers are a man of honor. All the seeds I gave last year were dead." He then banished his other eight sons for dishonoring his name.

IDEA #17

Multicultural Faire

> **OVERVIEW:** Within the context of a faire celebrating the class or school's cultural variety, students learn how to respect differences and embrace diversity.
>
> **PREPARATION / MATERIALS:**
> ● organizing the faire

A talent is formed in stillness, a character in the world's torrent.

— Johann Wolfgang von Goethe
German poet, dramatist, novelist and scientist (1749-1832)

PROCEDURE:

This activity will expose students to many different cultures and nurture in them a tolerance for diversity. Have them begin by researching their family history. Tell them to ask their parents where their ancestors came from and what some of the customs in their native culture are. Have students create a family tree and prepare a brief report about their cultural roots. Have them bring in an object from their culture for show-and-tell. As a culminating activity, hold a Multicultural Faire. Have students come to school in the traditional costume of their ancestors, and bring in a food from their culture to share with everyone.

Instruct students on how to demonstrate respect during the faire. For instance, tell them not to make fun of somebody's clothes or say their food is gross. During the faire, model respect by complimenting every child with a phrase such as "Your costume is very attractive," "This food is delicious!" or "How fascinating!" After the faire, discuss (or have students write about) the experience and how it felt to be surrounded by all the different cultures. Ask what similarities there were.

IDEA #18

Globingo

OVERVIEW: Students become aware of their classmates' diverse backgrounds and experiences, and earn recognition for their own.

PREPARATION / MATERIALS:
- Globingo card for each student
- map of the world (on the wall or on an overhead projector)
- pushpins

PROCEDURE:

This activity is ideal at the start of the school year, when students are just getting to know each other. Each box on the Globingo card describes a trait with an international flavor, such as "Enjoys music from another country," and students find classmates who fit each description on the card. The game encourages social interaction and draws attention to everyone's unique experiences and backgrounds.

Distribute the Globingo cards to students. Tell them they have 20 minutes (or more, at your discretion) to locate classmates who fit each description and have them sign the card. Advise students that they must ask each other questions, not just tell each other what box they can sign. Also, inform students that they can get each person's signature only once. The goal is to fill the card with signatures and learn about each other. Remind students to be respectful when asking questions.

After completing this exercise, call on volunteers to say who signed for particular descriptions, and ask them what country applied. On a map of the world, mark each country named with a pushpin or a sticky note. If students name a country more than once, mark it more than once. (You could also have a transparency map of the world on the overhead and mark countries with a pen, or have students mark the countries.) Ask students: *Did anything you discover about your classmates surprise you? What country is most common among all of us? What country is least common? Why is it important to respect everyone's differences?*

*I**f you never learn the language of gratitude you'll never be on speaking terms with happiness.*

— Unknown

Many websites offer similar lessons. See http://www.globalschools.org.uk/resources/globingo.htm, http://www.woodcraft.org.uk/resources/community/cm-glob.htm, and http://www.yhgsa.org.uk/resources/globingo.doc.

Globingo

Has traveled to a foreign country _____ Name _____ Country	Has received a letter or postcard from someone in another country _____ Name _____ Country	Can speak a language besides English _____ Name _____ Language
Enjoys music from another country _____ Name _____ Country	Is wearing something made in another country _____ Name _____ Country	Enjoys eating foods from other countries _____ Name _____ Country
Can name a famous person from another country _____ Name _____ Country	Learned something about another country on TV recently _____ Name _____ Country	Was born in another country _____ Name _____ Country
Has helped a visitor from another country _____ Name _____ Country	Has a family car that was made in another country _____ Name _____ Country	Has a relative born in, or now living in, another country _____ Name _____ Country

IDEA #19

Cause and Effect

> **OVERVIEW:** Students examine different scenarios, determine the options for action in each one, then analyze the effects of that action.
>
> **PREPARATION / MATERIALS:**
> none

PROCEDURE:

To be responsible, people need to foresee the consequences of their actions. In other words, they have to understand cause and effect. Present students with the scenarios listed below, and then ask students to list their choices and the possible effects of each one. If necessary, lead students to the suggested answers ("likely effects").

Scenarios:

1. You are playing baseball and hit a ball toward third. The third-baseman throws to first and you know you are out, but the umpire — an older kid — calls you safe. Players on the other team object and ask you whether you thought you were safe. What do you do?

Possible Choices
- Admit you were out.

Likely Effects
- Your team may have less of a chance to win the game.
- Some players on your team may wish you had lied, to improve their chances of winning.
- Players on both sides will respect your integrity.
- People will be more apt to trust you later, when your word may really matter.
- If you do win, you'll have the satisfaction of knowing you did it fair and square.

While we are free to choose our actions, we are not free to choose the consequences of our actions.

— Stephen Covey
Author, consultant and motivational speaker

Possible Choices

- Either say you don't know or claim you were safe.

Likely Effects

- Your team may have a greater chance to win the game.
- Some players on your team may be happy you've improved their chances of winning.
- Players on both sides will think you are a liar.
- Players will remember your lie long past the game itself, and will be more suspicious of you.
- The next time your word matters, people will be less likely to trust you.
- If you win, you may have the empty feeling of knowing you didn't deserve the victory.
- You may find it easier to lie next time.

2. The teacher assigns you a report on trees. You plan to write it on the night before it is due. That afternoon your parents say they're going to a fun place for dinner and ask if you want to come. You know that if you go, you won't be able to finish the report.

Possible Choices

- Tell your parents you have homework, stay home and finish the report on trees

Likely Effects

- You miss a fun dinner.
- You turn in your report on time.
- Your teacher is happy.
- Your parents are impressed.
- You feel good that you met the deadline and pleased your teacher and parents.

- Go out to dinner with your parents and the next day tell the teacher you forgot about the report.

- You have fun at the dinner, though you worry the whole time about the lie you'll tell tomorrow.
- Your teacher is upset that you did not turn in your work on time.
- You get a bad grade.
- Your parents are upset when they find out.
- You are grounded and aren't allowed to go outside, watch TV or play video games for two weeks.

IDEA #20

Emergency Preparedness

OVERVIEW: Students make a list of items to have on hand in case of an emergency, and perform drills at school.

PREPARATION / MATERIALS:
none

PROCEDURE:

Whether it's an earthquake, tornado, flood, fire or other disaster, everyone needs to know how to prepare for, and respond during, an emergency. A responsible person thinks ahead, anticipating reasonably likely events.

Have students brainstorm all the items they might need in an emergency, while you write the list on the board. Help them by asking, *What do you do at home when the electricity goes out. How do you get light? How do you (or your parents) cook food? What might you need in case someone is injured?*

When the emergency item list is complete, have students copy it down and take it home for their families to use in putting together an emergency preparedness kit. If your school lacks emergency preparedness kits for individual classrooms or the whole school, request parent donations to create them.

Throughout the year, conduct not only fire drills, but also other kinds, such as earthquake or tornado drills, depending on the disaster your region is more prone to. The more you emphasize preparedness, the more students understand that responsibility can save lives.

For more information about emergency preparedness, see the online booklet from FEMA (Federal Emergency Management Agency) or print it for free at http://www.fema.gov/areyouready/.

One of the tests of leadership is the ability to recognize a problem before it becomes an emergency.

— **Arnold Glasow**
American humorist

IDEA #21

Fairness Acrostic

OVERVIEW: To reinforce what being fair really means, students compose an acrostic.

PREPARATION / MATERIALS:
none

PROCEDURE:

Have students write FAIRNESS vertically on a sheet of paper. Then ask them to write a sentence about an example of fairness that starts with each letter. The lines need not rhyme. Students can also compose the acrostic in groups of three or four, or the whole class can do it together. Here is a sample acrostic:

F ollowing the rules in a game is the only fair way to play.
A sking the teacher for special treatment is not fair.
I t is fair to take turns washing the dishes.
R eally listening to others' opinions is necessary to be fair.
N obody should be blamed for something they didn't do.
E quality and fairness are not the same.
S ometimes, for example, you deserve more allowance because you work harder than your brother.
S haring with others inspires others to share with you.

Note: Students can also compose acrostics from any of the other Six Pillars: trustworthiness, respect, responsibility, caring or citizenship.

*Y*ou will become

as small as your

controlling desire,

as great as your

dominant

aspiration.

— James Allen
English writer
(1864-1912)

IDEA #22

Change the Rules

OVERVIEW: Students change the rules to well-known games, to make them fairer.

PREPARATION / MATERIALS:
- playing cards
- board games

PROCEDURE:

Children often change the rules in games to make them seem fairer. For example, in the card game Go Fish, the rule says you need four of a kind to claim them as a set and put them safely aside, but you can also make one pair a set. This could be seen as fairer because it gives more players a chance to get sets, and having to hand over three of a kind when you've taken the time to accumulate them can be seen as unfair.

Have students work in pairs or groups of four. Tell them to pick a game they want to play, either a card game everyone knows (you can't change the rules if you don't know them) or a board game from the stack. Tell students to change the rules of the game to make them fairer.

Extension:
Have students make up completely new rules using the same game board and game pieces. To determine if the rules are clear and fair, have students teach the game to another group and let that group decide.

Failure to hit the bull's-eye is never the fault of the target.

— attributed to Gilbert Arland

IDEA #23

Compliment Jar

OVERVIEW: Students draw the name of a classmate from the Compliment Jar and say one nice thing about that student.

PREPARATION / MATERIALS:
- empty and clean glass (or plastic) jar
- small slips of paper

The noblest service comes from nameless hands, and the best servant does his work unseen.

— **Oliver Wendell Holmes, Sr.**
Physician, poet and humorist
(1809-1894)

PROCEDURE:

Discuss with students the many different ways they can be caring towards a classmate. Direct them to identify acts that show compassion, consideration, kindness and charity.

Write the name of each student on a small slip of paper (about the size of a fortune in a fortune cookie), and place them all in the jar. Have children sit on the floor in a circle and pass the jar around. Each student then draws a slip and pays a compliment to the person whose name is on it.

Alternately, students can perform a random act of kindness for that individual later in the day.

_____

● read up and reach out at www.charactercounts.org ●

IDEA #24

IALAC Tags

OVERVIEW: After reading *I Am Lovable and Capable* by Sidney Simon, students create their own IALAC tags and wear them. They tear off a piece when they receive a negative comment, and color a section or add a sticker when they receive a positive comment.

PREPARATION / MATERIALS:
- copy of *I Am Lovable and Capable* by Sidney Simon
- blank 8½" x 11" paper cut in half, or 5" x 7" index cards
- crayons or markers
- hole puncher
- yarn or string, one 20" segment for each student
- stickers (optional)

PROCEDURE:

Read the story *I Am Lovable and Capable* (IALAC) by Sidney Simon out loud to students. Discuss the impact of positive and negative comments on people's feelings and self-esteem.

Have students create IALAC tags to wear around their necks for one day. Hand out markers and either half sheets of white paper or 5" x 7" index cards. Have students write their names on the cards, along with the acronym "IALAC." Pass the hole puncher around and have students punch two holes in the top of the card, one in the upper left corner and one in the upper right. Then pass out the string and have students tie the ends through the holes in the cards.

Students should wear the cards around their necks for one whole school day. When they hear a positive comment aimed at them, they color a section of the tag, or add a sticker. If they hear a negative comment directed toward them, they tear off a piece of the tag. At the end of the day, students reflect either in discussion or in a journal on the state of their own cards and the cards of others, and what that means about the caring (or lack thereof) that was demonstrated.

Consider having students make tags the next day as well, and see if the tags are in better condition at the end of the second day than the first.

Note: Some students may jokingly make negative comments to purposely destroy someone's tag. Use this as a teachable moment to show how joking can be just as hurtful as real teasing or bullying.

Adapted from an idea in the Character Sketches December 2000 newsletter, a publication of the University of Nebraska – Lincoln (see http://character.sketches.unl.edu/cs22001.pdf) which was in turn inspired by the book I Am Lovable and Capable *by Sidney Simon.*

The happiness of life is made up of minute fractions — the little soon-forgotten charities of a kiss or smile, a kind look, a heartfelt compliment, and the countless infinitesimals of pleasurable and genial feeling.

— Samuel Taylor Coleridge
English poet
(1772-1834)

IDEA #25

Class Elections

> **OVERVIEW:** Students participate in class elections throughout the year, both as candidates and as voters.
>
> **PREPARATION / MATERIALS:**
> none

A man of character will make himself worthy of any position he is given.

— Mahatma Gandhi
Indian social activist and philosopher
(1869-1948)

PROCEDURE:

Both running for an office — essentially volunteering to serve — and voting are acts of citizenship. Neither is required but both benefit the common good.

If you do not already have class elections for positions such as president, vice president and historian, create them. You can also turn any classroom job into an elected position, including line leader, paper collector, paper returner and messenger.

If you already have elections, hold them multiple times throughout the year by making the term of service one or two months rather than a whole semester or year. Benefits of this approach include:

- letting more students run for election and serve in office
- increasing the number of chances students have to vote
- requiring students to face opponents at reelection time, where they can learn firsthand about fair campaigning

This exercise is especially relevant during a presidential election year, but it is useful at any time.

IDEA #26

Design a Bumper Sticker or T-Shirt

OVERVIEW: Students design their own bumper sticker with a catchy slogan, or T-shirt with colorful art, to promote their favorite cause.

PREPARATION / MATERIALS:
- blank paper cut in strips, bumper sticker size
- paper with T-shirt outline
- crayons or markers

PROCEDURE:

Getting the message out about a good cause is part of being a good citizen. Either ask students to pick a cause, or relate a cause to topics you are studying, such as the environment, homeless animals, world hunger, child abuse or disaster relief. Have students design a bumper sticker with a catchy slogan or a T-shirt with a colorful design (or both!) to promote the cause. Tell students that the bumper sticker or T-shirt should grab people's attention, so they become aware of the issue and are inspired to take action.

Extension: Stage a contest for the best bumper sticker and the best T-shirt, and have the winning designs produced as a fundraiser for your school in which half the proceeds go to a charity associated with the cause.

Note: If students choose to promote **CHARACTER COUNTS!** we would love to see their designs. Please send them to our national office at 9841 Airport Blvd., #300, Los Angeles, CA 90045.

From what we get, we can make a living; what we give, however, makes a life.

—Arthur Ashe
Professional tennis player and social activist (1943-1993)

IDEA #27

Flip Chart

> **OVERVIEW:** Students create a flip chart to remind them of the Six Pillars.
>
> **PREPARATION / MATERIALS:**
> - strips of blank paper, 11" x 4¼", four for each student
> - sample flip chart
> - crayons or markers
> - bank of character quotes (optional)

Virtue is harder to be got than a knowledge of the world; and, if lost in a young man, is seldom recovered.

— John Locke
English philosopher
(1632-1704)

PROCEDURE:

A flip chart is a study tool that helps students organize and review information on any topic. Here, students create a flip chart for the Six Pillars. Each Pillar has its own page and comes with an explanation of it in the student's own words, as well as pictures to illustrate it.

To make a flip chart, give each student four strips of paper measuring 11" by 4¼". (Make strips by cutting a standard sheet of white paper in half the long way.) Have students lay the first strip vertically on their desk. Then place the second strip on top of it, but leave a half inch of the bottom strip showing. Repeat this procedure twice more, until four strips lie on the desk. Then have students pick up the strips all at once, keeping them neatly arranged, and fold the top over so that there are eight pages showing, each one progressively longer than the one above it. Have students staple the flip chart at the top, as close to the fold as possible. It helps to display a sample flip chart to illustrate this process. See the next page for an instructional diagram.

The top strip will serve as both cover and title page. Have students label the bottom of each following page with the name of a Pillar. For consistency, we suggest writing them in order: Trustworthiness, Respect, Responsibility, Fairness, Caring, Citizenship. (Students may wish to write them in their corresponding colors: Trustworthiness: blue, Respect: yellow, Responsibility: green, Fairness: orange, Caring: red, Citizenship: purple.) Then on each labeled page, ask students to describe what that Pillar means to them, and draw a picture symbolizing the Pillar.

Students can either leave the final page blank or write a character quote of their choice. See http://www.josephsoninstitute.org/quotes/quotetoc.htm (and the margins of this book) for many character-related quotations.

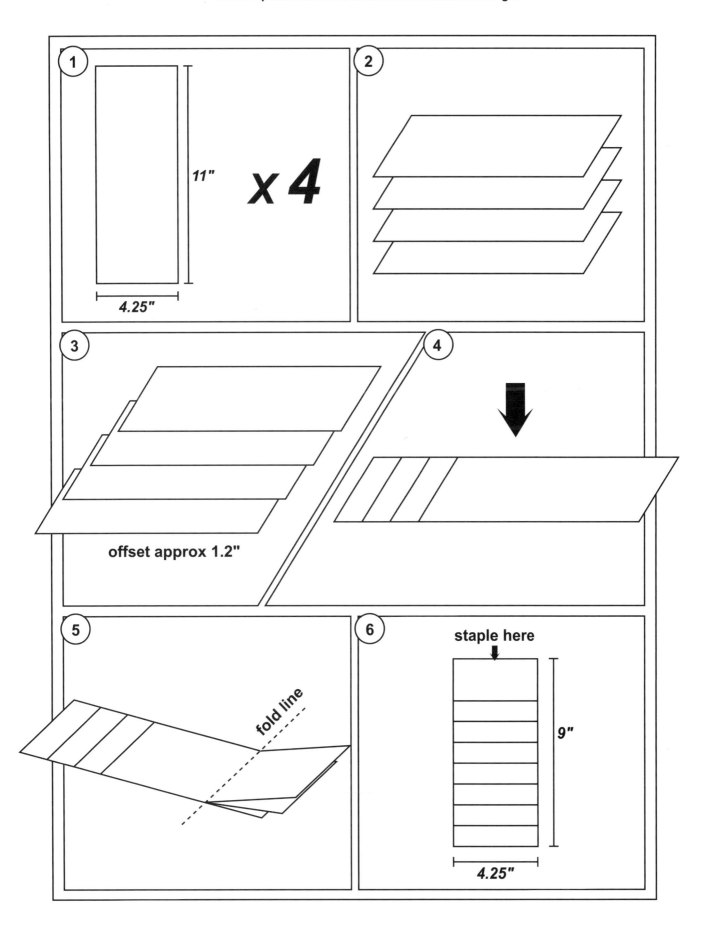

1

11"

x 4

4.25"

2

3

offset approx 1.2"

4

5

fold line

6

staple here

9"

4.25"

IDEA #28

Six Pillar Memory

OVERVIEW: Students play the classic card game Memory but with a Six Pillars twist. Children can create their own cards or use teacher-prepared ones.

PREPARATION / MATERIALS:
- sheet of Memory cards, one for each pair of students
- crayons or markers
- scissors
- envelopes or zipper baggies to store cards

Character, not circumstance, makes the person.

— Booker T. Washington
American educator and civil rights activist (1856-1915)

PROCEDURE:

One or two people can play Six Pillar Memory. The goal is to obtain the most matching sets. A matching set consists of two cards, one with the name of the Pillar and a second with an illustration representing that Pillar.

Make sets of cards by photocopying the next page. (The children can also create their own cards.) Be sure there are enough copies for each pair of students to have a set of cards. Distribute card sheets, scissors and coloring implements. Have students color the cards, cut them out and place each card set in its own envelope or zipper baggie. (Note: If the cards will be used more than once, we recommend copying on heavier paper stock or gluing the sheet of cards to construction paper before cutting. In addition to adding durability, this will also prevent the words and pictures from showing through the paper when turned over.)

Begin play. Mix up all the cards and turn them upside down on the desk. Students turn over a card, then try to find the match to that card by turning over one more card. If they match, the student picks them up and puts them on his or her side of the desk. If they don't match, both cards get turned over again in the same spot and it is the next player's turn. After all matches are made, the student with the most cards wins.

read up and reach out at www.charactercounts.org

THE SIX PILLARS OF CHARACTER

TRUSTWORTHINESS
- Be honest.
- Don't deceive, cheat or steal.
- Be reliable — do what you say you'll do.
- Have the courage to do the right thing.
- Build a good reputation.
- Be loyal — stand by your family, friends and country.

RESPECT
- Treat others with respect; follow the Golden Rule.
- Be tolerant of differences.
- Use good manners, not bad language.
- Be considerate of the feelings of others.
- Don't threaten, hit or hurt anyone.
- Deal peacefully with anger, insults and disagreements.

RESPONSIBILITY
- Do what you are supposed to do.
- Persevere: keep on trying!
- Always do your best.
- Use self-control.
- Be self-disciplined.
- Think before you act — consider the consequences.
- Be accountable for your choices.

FAIRNESS
- Play by the rules.
- Take turns and share.
- Be open-minded; listen to others.
- Don't take advantage of others.
- Don't blame others carelessly.

CARING
- Be kind.
- Be compassionate; show you care.
- Express gratitude.
- Forgive others.
- Help people in need.

CITIZENSHIP
- Do your share to make your school and community better.
- Cooperate.
- Stay informed; vote.
- Be a good neighbor.
- Obey laws and rules.
- Respect authority.
- Protect the environment

GOOD IDEAS

to Help <u>9- to 11-Year-Olds</u> Develop Good Character

IDEA #29

Classroom Library

> **OVERVIEW:** Students learn to demonstrate trustworthy behavior through borrowing books.
>
> **PREPARATION / MATERIALS:**
> - lightly used books
> - bookshelves
> - tracking sheet

Integrity without knowledge is weak and useless, and knowledge without integrity is dangerous and dreadful.

— Samuel Johnson
English author
(1709-1784)

PROCEDURE:

If you don't have a classroom library, begin one by asking students to donate lightly used books. Write your name in each book (or use nameplates). Put someone in charge of keeping the books arranged neatly on the shelves. Another student, the "librarian," will use a simple chart to track who has checked out which books and until when. (You may want the class to elect students for these positions — see Idea #25.)

Tell students: *When you borrow something, you make a promise to return it at a certain time in the same condition or better. Keeping promises will earn you the reputation of being trustworthy.*

Although students also have access to the public library, it is less personal and when students don't see firsthand the effects of untrustworthiness, they can more easily rationalize it. A classroom library makes the borrowing experience more immediate and highlights the fact that others suffer if a book is lost or damaged.

When students check out books, say to them, *I am trusting that you will return these books on or before the due date and in the same condition as they're in now. Are you trustworthy?* Students should say they are. If they prove untrustworthy, enforce penalties such as having them miss recess or dismissing them last for lunch. If a student repeatedly is untrustworthy, revoke his or her library privileges.

Classroom Library Tracking Sheet

Date	Student Name	Book Title	Due Date

IDEA #30

Dishonesty in TV Shows

OVERVIEW: Students keep a log of each time honesty or dishonesty plays a role in a TV show.

PREPARATION / MATERIALS:
- copy of TV log, one for each student
- letter home to parents about TV project, one for each student

Mine honour

is my life; both

grow in one; Take

honour from me,

and my life is done.

— William Shakespeare
English playwright
and poet
(1564-1616)

PROCEDURE:

In drama, dishonesty is a classic plot device to set up action or move it along. For instance, children lie to their parents, employees lie to their bosses, spouses lie to each other. Deception was the very premise of the old TV show "Bosom Buddies," in which two men pretended to be women so they could live in a women's-only apartment building. These days, with the popularity of reality shows, dishonesty has proliferated. The ends are often used to justify the means and it seems acceptable to lie, cheat, and deceive one's way to victory.

For one week (or more) have students keep a log of each time honesty or dishonesty plays a role in a TV show they are watching. Send a letter home to parents so that they know that watching TV is part of this assignment. Afterwards, have students get into groups and compare logs. Ask students: *How many of you logged the same incidents? Are there one or two shows which appear on almost everyone's log? What message does this programming send about what people find entertaining? What are the consequences of this dishonesty? Are these dishonest characters good role models?*

Inspired by an idea briefly mentioned in the teaching guide for the video Trustworthiness *in the series* The Six Pillars of Character *(produced by Live Wire Media and available at www.charactercounts.org).*

● read up and reach out at www.charactercounts.org ●

Honesty (and Dishonesty) in TV Shows

Date	Time	Name of TV Show	Honesty	Dishonesty	Description

Date:_____

Dear Parents,

As you may know, trustworthiness is one of the Six Pillars of Character that our school promotes as part of our **CHARACTER COUNTS!** program. A key aspect of trustworthiness is honesty, and children need role models to help them integrate honesty into their daily lives. Unfortunately, the media often provide role models who engage in untrustworthy behavior, especially in the "reality" shows.

For the next week, our class will be working on a project to analyze TV shows for honesty and dishonesty. Your child will need to watch between 30 and 60 minutes of television per night. You have complete discretion about the programs they view. If you prefer to prerecord shows you feel are appropriate, by all means do so. However, there is also merit in letting students see the level of dishonesty in average nightly programming. You can use this project as a springboard for discussion about honesty and trustworthiness. We will also be discussing this at length in class.

Thank you for your support with this assignment.

Sincerely,

_____

IDEA #31

What Is Tact?

OVERVIEW: Students learn through different scenarios that sometimes honesty can be brutal, so tact is necessary.

PREPARATION / MATERIALS:
- copy of tact handout for each student or pair of students

PROCEDURE:

As a general rule, honesty is the best policy. However, the truth is not always pretty, and sometimes blunt honesty can be hurtful. Introduce *tact* as a new vocabulary word, meaning honesty that could be viewed as criticism but which is carefully worded in consideration of the other person's feelings. In other words, if you are saying something that could upset a person, use tact. Tact, though truthful, is not insulting or rude. The art of tact involves phrasing things to avoid hurt feelings and provide constructive criticism.

Give students examples of tact:

Situation	Rude Response	Tactful Response
Your friend asks you, "Do you like my new coat?"	"No, it's ugly."	"It is not my style but it looks good on you."
Your friend asks if you want to go to the park together.	"I don't really like playing with you."	"I don't really feel like it, but thank you for the invitation."
Your teacher asks if you enjoyed reading your book	"No, it was dumb and boring."	"Not really but I know reading is good for me."

Advise students that in each situation, there is the potential for hurt feelings or anger. But by emphasizing the positive, and offering solutions for the negative, you can provide tactfully honest answers that do not offend anyone.

Distribute the tact handout and have students complete it individually or in pairs. They are to come up with possible responses to each scenario, dealing with the situations honestly, but considerately.

We live in a world which is full of misery and ignorance, and the plain duty of each and all of us is to try to make the little corner he can influence somewhat less miserable and somewhat less ignorant than it was before he entered it.

— Thomas Henry Huxley
English biologist
(1825-1895)

Tact

Think of a tactful way to respond in each situation. Remember, using tact means you are still honest, but you use your words carefully to avoid hurting someone's feelings.

1. For Christmas, your grandmother gives you a sweatshirt which you think is ugly. She asks how you like it. What should you say?

   _____

   _____

2. You are watching TV and the phone rings. Your mom answers it and tells you it's Jane. You don't like Jane and don't want to talk to her. What should you say?

   _____

   _____

3. Your friend gets a new baby sister and you think it is the ugliest baby you've ever seen. Your friend asks you, "Isn't she the cutest?" What should you say?

   _____

   _____

4. Your teacher is walking down the hallway with a piece of trash stuck to her shoe heel. What should you say?

   _____

   _____

5. Your friend has been talking for 10 minutes with a big piece of broccoli stuck between his teeth. What should you say?

   _____

   _____

6. You are visiting your friend's house and your friend's mom serves liver and onions for dinner, which you think is disgusting. What should you say?

   _____

   _____

IDEA #32

Standing Up for Diversity

OVERVIEW: Students stand when they agree with certain statements, illustrating the diversity of all classmates. A discussion follows emphasizing everyone's agreement on the importance of respect.

PREPARATION / MATERIALS:
none

PROCEDURE:

Read the following statements out loud and ask students to stand after each one if they agree with it. (If a student cannot stand, have everyone respond instead by raising their hands.) You may wish to keep a tally on the board of how many students agree with each statement.

- I like the color pink.
- I believe one should resolve conflicts peacefully if possible.
- I like the color blue.
- I like it when others use good manners.
- I am a meat lover.
- I am a vegetable lover.
- I am a "morning person."
- I am glad the world is full of different types of people.
- I was born on the West Coast.
- I believe one should be considerate of others' feelings.
- I was born in the Midwest.
- I like it when others have good manners.
- I was born in a country outside the United States.
- I am the oldest child in my family.
- I do not believe it is all right to hit, threaten or hurt someone else.
- I am a middle child in my family.
- I am the youngest in my family.
- I like to be valued as a person.

Discussion questions:

- How are your classmates different from you?
- How are your classmates similar to you?

Feeling gratitude and not expressing it is like wrapping a present and not giving it.

— William Arthur Ward
American college administrator
(1921-1994)

- What questions did the majority, if not all, of your classmates agree on?
- Which Pillars related to the statement(s) that most, if not all, of your classmates agreed on?

This lesson illustrates how, regardless of diversity—and because of it—respect is an important Pillar for every student.

Submitted by Dr. Mark J. Britzman, Professor of Counseling and Human Resource Development at South Dakota State University.

IDEA #33

Establishing Priorities

OVERVIEW: Students learn how to prioritize tasks and achieve their goals more efficiently.

PREPARATION / MATERIALS:
- copy of "How to Prioritize Responsibilities," one for each student

PROCEDURE:

Conscientious students sometimes feel overwhelmed when it comes to managing their responsibilities if they do not know how to prioritize.

Introduce *priority* and *prioritize* as vocabulary words. Say, *A priority is something that is very important and must get more of your attention sooner. Everyone has different priorities. For example, one of the president's top priorities is the safety of the American people. A very low priority for him is what's for dinner. But if you are having an important guest over, what's for dinner can be a fairly high priority. When you prioritize, you put things in order of most important to least important. You have to prioritize if you have lots of things to do and don't know where to start. To be responsible, you must get to all of them, but some will be more important than others.*

Distribute copies of "How to Prioritize Responsibilities" to students. This handout lists seven criteria for prioritizing. Each criterion offers a different perspective from which to view tasks. First, have students make a to-do list with four tasks on it, in no particular order. The list can be real or made up. Then have them complete the handout, putting the list in order of priority for each criterion. The lists may (and should) be different from criterion to criterion, showing the complexity of making these decisions. For example, a task may be very urgent—say, an assignment that is due tomorrow—so it would be #1 on the deadlines list, but not personally important to the student, so it would be #4 on that one. Then tell students, *Taking into consideration all the different ways you can prioritize, make a final decision about the order you should complete your own to-do list.* Call on volunteers to explain their rationales behind how they chose to prioritize.

Again and again, the impossible problem is solved when we see that the problem is only a tough decision waiting to be made.

— Robert H. Schuller
Christian minister, author and motivational speaker (b. 1926)

Adapted from a lesson titled, "How Can You Decide Among Competing Responsibilities?" posted on http://www.civnet.org/resources/teach/lessplan/responsb.htm.

read up and reach out at www.charactercounts.org

How to Prioritize Responsibilities

First, you must identify your responsibilities. Make a list of "things to do."

My list of things to do in no particular order:

1. _____   3. _____

2. _____   4. _____

Then, consider that list from each of the following points of view, and re-order your to-do list accordingly.

A. Consequences. Ask yourself: *What are the good things that will happen if I complete a task? What are the bad things that will happen if I don't complete it?* Tasks with strong positive or negative consequences should come first.

My to-do list prioritized by consequences:

1. _____   3. _____

2. _____   4. _____

B. Deadlines. Ask yourself: *How urgent is each task? When must each task be completed?* Tasks with earlier deadlines should come first.

My to-do list prioritized by deadlines:

1. _____   3. _____

2. _____   4. _____

C. Importance. Ask yourself: *If I stand back and look at the "big picture," what task matters most, second most, and so on?*

My to-do list prioritized by importance:

1. _____   3. _____

2. _____   4. _____

D. Time needed. Ask yourself: *What are the steps I have to take to complete each task, and how long will they take me? Are there quick things I can get out of the way first? Or should I get big projects done first?*

My to-do list prioritized by time needed:

1. _____   3. _____

2. _____   4. _____

E. Resources. Ask yourself: *Do I have everything I need to complete the task? If not, how easily can I get what I need?* Tasks you are prepared for and able to do now should go first on this list. (Keep in mind, however, that if you are not able to get started on something it is important to get prepared as soon as possible.)

My to-do list prioritized by resources:

1. _____ 3. _____

2. _____ 4. _____

F. Personal value. Ask yourself: *How much does each task matter to me personally? Is one near and dear to my heart, while another is not?* Tasks that matter to you most should come first on this list.

My to-do list prioritized by personal value:

1. _____ 3. _____

2. _____ 4. _____

G. Alternate solution. Ask yourself: *Are there any compromises that will eliminate one of my tasks? Can I "cross two hurdles with one leap" somehow?* For example, suppose you have a Little League practice, <u>and</u> you have to finish your homework. Solution: take your homework to the game and work on it in the dugout while you are waiting for your turn at bat. Tasks you can compromise on should come first on this list.

My to-do list prioritized by possible alternate solutions:

1. _____ 3. _____

2. _____ 4. _____

My final to-do list:

1. _____ 3. _____

2. _____ 4. _____

Adapted from http://www.civnet.org/resources/teach/lessplan/responsb.htm.

read up and reach out at www.charactercounts.org

IDEA #34

Career Day

> **OVERVIEW:** Within the context of a general Career Day, students compare the responsibilities of several different professions.
>
> **PREPARATION / MATERIALS:**
> - letter to presenters
> - copies of Venn diagrams or T-charts for each student

The pursuit of excellence is less profitable than the pursuit of bigness, but it can be more satisfying.

— David Ogilvy
Advertising executive
and author
(1911-1999)

PROCEDURE:

Career Days generally focus on professions children can follow when they grow up and the rewards for each. This activity encourages students to look at professions in terms of what *responsibilities* each one requires.

Notify the Career Day presenters in advance (see sample letter provided) that students will be looking for detailed information about job obligations, and encourage presenters to bring visual aids—such as overhead transparencies, posters and handouts—to illustrate the main duties.

Before the big Career Day, have students get ready by researching various occupations. This will prepare students for the type of questions they will be asking presenters at Career Day. Coach students to look at the jobs analytically by comparing and contrasting their responsibilities. After the presentations, have students select two occupations in which they are especially interested, and complete a Venn diagram if the two jobs have overlapping duties. Otherwise, students can fill out a T-chart with the different duties of each position.

Extensions:

- Have students write a paragraph about which job they would prefer and why.
- Discuss what life would be like if no one wanted to live up to the responsibilities in demanding jobs like law enforcement, emergency response and teaching.

Note: If your school does not have an organized a Career Day, and you do not desire to plan one yourself, this activity can still be used independently as an occupation research project.

● read up and reach out at www.charactercounts.org ●

Dear Presenter,

Thank you for agreeing to participate in our school's Career Day. Your presentation will help get students thinking about their futures and the steps they need to take to fulfill their dreams.

In addition to presenting general information about your profession, we would like you to describe your job responsibilities in some detail. Responsibility is one of the **CHARACTER COUNTS!** Six Pillars, and although the rewards of a job may be more glamorous than its duties, we want students to focus on the responsibilities in each job. After Career Day, we will ask students to compare and contrast the responsibilities of two or more professions.

If possible, please bring a visual aid—such as an overhead transparency, poster, or photocopied handout—with your major responsibilities clearly listed. (If you bring a handout, note that we have _____ students.)

If you have any further questions about Career Day, please feel free to call me at _____ any time.

Sincerely,

_____

read up and reach out at www.charactercounts.org

CAREER ONE   CAREER TWO

_____   _____

_____   _____

_____   _____

_____   _____

_____   _____

_____   _____

_____   _____

_____   _____

_____   _____

_____   _____

_____   _____

● read up and reach out at www.charactercounts.org ●

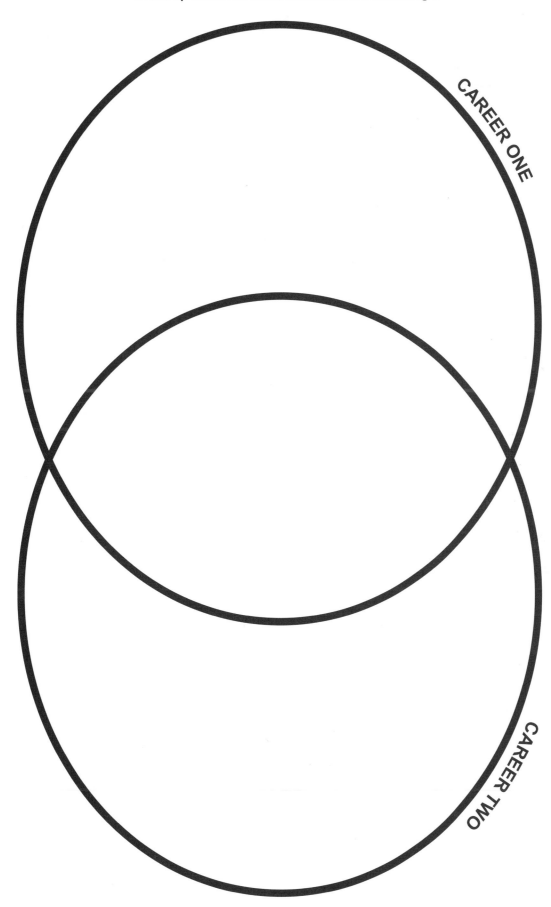

CAREER ONE

CAREER TWO

IDEA #35

Fact vs. Opinion

OVERVIEW: Students look for bias in the media and write their own news stories (about school or local events) without interpretation, only observation.

PREPARATION / MATERIALS:
- copy of editorial on a given topic, one for each student
- copy of news story on same topic as editorial, one for each student
- copies of news magazines or newspapers (optional)
- highlighters (optional)

PROCEDURE:

News stories are supposed to be impartial. They should report only facts, not opinion, and should never lead the reader to take a certain side on issues. However, often facts mix with the opinions of the reporter, editor, or newspaper in a way that indicates bias.

Distribute copies of the news story and editorial that you have selected on the same topic. Have students read both silently (or call on volunteers) and then ask, *Which article had only facts? Which article had both facts and opinions?* Chances are both articles will have facts and opinions; the opinions will be subtle in the news article, but obvious in the editorial.

Have students write a news article about an event in your school or community. Remind them to use only factual information. Instruct them to include the Five W's: Who, What, When, Where and Why. Then have students exchange papers and read each other's articles looking for any trace of bias. If found, students should revise the article until it is free of opinions.

Extensions:
1. Have students write an editorial on the same topic as their school news story, encouraging them to state their opinions strongly *and* support them with facts.

2. Provide copies of newspapers and/or news magazines. Have students go on a scavenger hunt to find opinions in news articles. Challenge them to find the most opinions they can on one newspaper or magazine page. Students can circle the opinions, highlight them, or copy them down.

IDEA #36

From a Different Perspective

> **OVERVIEW:** Students read (or recall) common fairy tales and rewrite one from a different character's point of view.
>
> **PREPARATION / MATERIALS:**
> - book of fairy tales
> - photocopy of fairy tale template, one (or more) for each student

PROCEDURE:

Children have a heightened awareness of fairness, yet they are often oblivious to the fact that what seems fair to them is not fair to all parties involved.

Introduce the concept of perspective. Tell students, *A perspective is a way of looking at something or thinking about it. People often have different perspectives even if they are looking at or thinking about the same thing. For example, if you stand in front of a statue, you have a different perspective than someone standing behind it. Likewise, people who love to read have a different perspective on raising taxes for a new library than people who rarely read.*

Read several fairy tales to the students, or call on volunteers to retell the stories in their own words. Distribute the fairy tale template handout and tell students to pick one story to rewrite from a nontraditional point of view:

- "Three Little Pigs" and "Little Red Riding Hood": from the wolf's perspective
- "Jack and the Beanstalk": from the giant's perspective
- "Snow White" and "Sleeping Beauty": from the witch's perspective
- "Cinderella": from a stepsister's perspective

Call on volunteers to read their revised stories. Then discuss how the stories differed depending on whose perspective they were told from. Ask, *Is one version of a story more fair than the other? Or does someone's idea of fairness depend on how they look at the situation?*

The choices that make a significant difference in our lives are the tough ones. They're not often fun or easy, but they're the ones we have to make, and each is a deliberate step toward better understanding who we really are.

— Alexandra Stoddard
Interior decorator, author and lecturer

read up and reach out at www.charactercounts.org

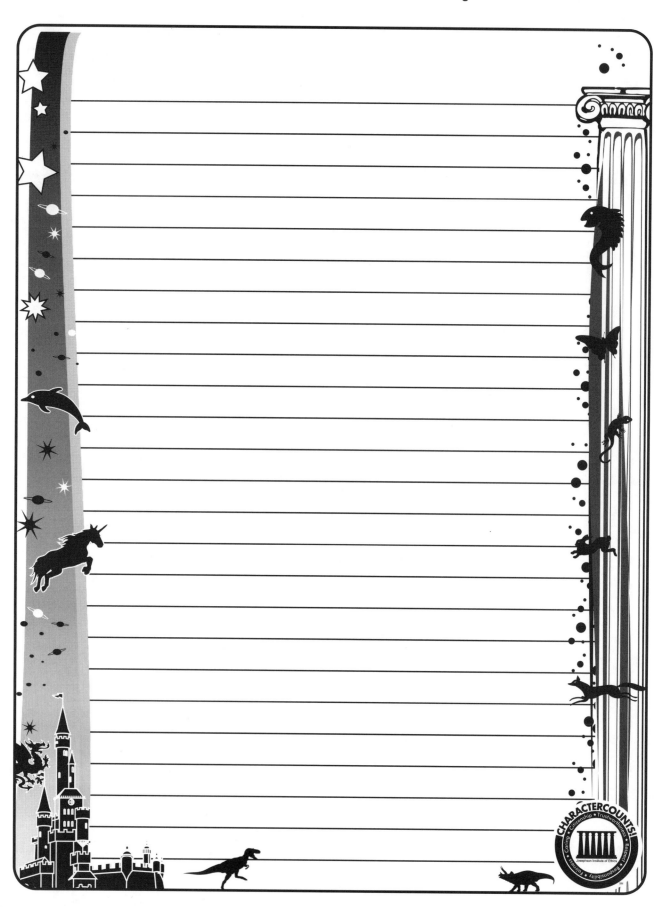

More Good Ideas to Help Young People Develop Good Character

©2004 Josephson Institute of Ethics

● read up and reach out at www.charactercounts.org ●

IDEA #37

Caring Commercial

> **OVERVIEW:** Using a video camera, students create a commercial about what it means to be caring in everyday life. If approached, a public-access TV station may run it.
>
> **PREPARATION / MATERIALS:**
> - video camera(s)
> - blank videotapes

PROCEDURE:

The law requires TV and radio stations to air a certain number of public service announcements on social issues like literacy, voting or avoiding drug abuse.

Tell students they will be making a public service commercial to promote caring. Students will work in groups to write a script. The commercial can consist of each student making a statement about caring in general, or of short skits showing examples of caring. The commercial should not be longer than 60 seconds. Groups can either get together on their own time and videotape the commercial, or they can perform it in front of the class as the teacher tapes them.

Extensions:

1. If your school has video announcements, air the best commercials during that time.
2. Make commercials for the other five Pillars.
3. Ask your community access cable channel to air the public service announcement. Sometimes these stations will even let school groups use their equipment to record such commercials.
4. A radio station may air the audio portion alone.
5. Have the commercials focus on one theme related to caring, such as bullying, teasing, compassion or charity.

*T*o know what is

right and not to do

it is the worst

cowardice.

— Confucius
Chinese philosopher
(551-479 B.C.)

IDEA #38

Life Lab

OVERVIEW: Students grow a garden and learn about the plant life cycle while learning to care for a growing organism.

PREPARATION / MATERIALS:
- gardening supplies (patch of land or large planter box, fertilizer, seeds, shovels, watering cans, etc.)
- Life Lab curriculum (optional)

Do what you

can with what

you have where

you are.

— **Theodore Roosevelt**
26th U.S. president,
author and
adventurer
(1858-1919)

PROCEDURE:

Nothing nurtures a child's sense of caring as much as taking care of a live, growing thing. The University of California, Santa Cruz houses a program called Life Lab, which helps schools develop gardens where children create "living laboratories" to study the natural world. You can implement a similar unit on a smaller scale. All you need are gardening materials and a small patch of land or a large planter box.

Have students plant varied vegetables and plants, and throughout the growth process stress the importance of caring for the living organism which will eventually nourish the caregiver. You can easily integrate this activity into a range of subjects, such as math (have students measure growth of plants), science (teach the life cycle of plants and environmental issues such as water conservation and use of pesticides), English (have students write about the experience), and history (indicate that the vast majority of people were farmers before the Industrial Revolution).

See Life Lab's website at http://www.lifelab.org/index.html for information on upcoming events and how to order curricular materials. A good introduction to the program can be found at http://www.valleywater.org/media/pdf/ACfall2003.pdf.

IDEA #39

Writing to Service Members

OVERVIEW: Students write letters of support for the men and women in uniform serving our country.

PREPARATION / MATERIALS:
- letter-writing stationery
- card-making supplies, such as construction paper, markers, ribbon, glitter, and glue
- envelopes
- overseas postage
- addresses of service members
- computer with Internet access (optional)
- small box (optional)
- care package items (optional)

PROCEDURE:

Regardless of political debates, the military men and women serving our country deserve our unqualified support. Ask if any students have relatives deployed overseas. If so, request that they bring in the mailing address so the class can send letters and perhaps even a care package. If no one in the class has a deployed relative, get the addresses of soldiers related to faculty members or friends. Otherwise, students can write e-mails to the troops in general at http://anyservicemember.navy.mil/, a service known as Operation Dear Abby.

Be sure to review students' messages not just for errors but for appropriateness. Discuss with students beforehand what kind of message a soldier would find encouraging. Both letters and cards are welcome, and cards can be handmade.

If the class is sending a package, see http://www.usmc-mccs.org/News/deploy/mailtotroops.asp for important guidelines. You can solicit care package donations from students, parents and even the whole school. Keep in mind that individual boxes must be small in size to be delivered.

Note: After September 11, the Department of Defense stopped forwarding personal care packages and correspondence addressed to "Any Service Member." Instead, the USO created "Operation USO Care Package." If your class does not have the address of a particular troop, but still wishes to donate a care package to a soldier, see http://www.usometrodc.org/care1.html.

Nothing is less worthy of honor than an old man who has no other evidence of having lived long except his age.

— Lucius Annaeus Seneca
Roman playwright
(c. 4 B.C.-65 A.D.)

IDEA #40

Citizenship Experiment

OVERVIEW: Students follow the scientific method to design and conduct an experiment on how often people break the laws on jaywalking and littering.

PREPARATION / MATERIALS:
- familiarity with the scientific method

PROCEDURE:

M en's minds are too ready to excuse guilt in themselves.

— Titus Livius
Roman historian and
philosopher
(59 B.C.-17 A.D.)

People must obey the law for society to remain orderly. Thus, good citizens comply with the laws. However, certain laws are often casually ignored.

After students are familiar with the scientific method (observe, question, hypothesize, predict, test, conclude), instruct them to create an experiment to gauge how often certain laws are broken, which laws are broken, and who breaks them.

First, based on their observations of the world, students should formulate a question, such as *How often do people litter? Which is more common, littering or jaywalking?* or *Who litters more, children or adults?* Next, have the class create a hypothesis to answer the question, such as: *People litter once every two minutes in the park* or *Children litter twice as often as adults.* Then have students construct an experiment to track how often those laws are broken, or who breaks them. Students should record their data in an organized manner, so they can easily analyze it later for a conclusion.

Once students finish collecting data, have them analyze it to answer the initial question and determine whether their hypothesis was correct.

Then discuss the implications of the results. Ask students, *Is casual violation of certain laws OK? Why or why not? Why do some people obviously think it is OK, as demonstrated by the behavior you observed? What if no one obeyed these laws? If the laws are insignificant, why do you suppose lawmakers enacted them? At what point does a law become so important that no one can ignore it?*

IDEA #41

Quote Scavenger Hunt

OVERVIEW: On the Internet, students search for meaningful, inspirational quotes on any given Pillar, or all six. They compile them into a booklet or write them on mini-posters to display around the room.

PREPARATION / MATERIALS:
- computers with Internet access
- blank paper, several sheets for each student
- crayons or markers
- scissors
- copy of quote scavenger hunt handout, one for each student

PROCEDURE:

Quotes can be powerful bits of wisdom that reinforce the message of the Six Pillars. The Josephson Institute (parent organization of CHARACTER COUNTS!) has assembled an extensive collection of character-related quotes on its website at http://www.josephsoninstitute.org/quotes/quotetoc.htm.

Distribute the Quote Scavenger Hunt handout and have students find quotes on each issue. Alternatively, have students search the quote database for their 10 favorite quotes related to one Pillar. Students can search other quote sites for additional quotations related to the Six Pillars.

After students complete the scavenger hunt or assemble their quote lists, have them create mini-booklets of their quotes, written neatly and decorated attractively. Students can also make mini-posters of their quotes and post them around the room.

Our deeds still travel with us from afar, And what we have been makes us what we are.

— George Eliot
English novelist
(1819-1880)

read up and reach out at www.charactercounts.org

Six Pillars Quote Scavenger Hunt

Pillar/Trait	Quote
Trustworthiness	
1. Honesty	
2. Integrity	
3. Loyalty	
4. Promise-keeping/Reliability	
Respect	
5. Tolerance	
6. Courtesy	
7. Patience	
Responsibility	
8. Accountability	
9. Self-control	
10. Pursuit of excellence	
Fairness	
11. Justice	
12. Equality	
13. Open-mindedness	

Pillar/Trait	Quote
Caring	
14. Generosity	
15. Love	
16. Compassion	
Citizenship	
17. Lawfulness	
18. Community service	
19. Patriotism	

IDEA #42

Six Pillars Passport

OVERVIEW: Students take a character self-assessment at the beginning of the school year, and as they journey through the world of the Six Pillars of Character, they get stamps in their "passports." At the end of the year, they reassess themselves to see how much they've improved.

PREPARATION / MATERIALS:
- copy of character self-assessment, one for each student
- teacher-made survey (optional)
- copy of passport, one for each student
- six different rubber stamps (relating to the Six Pillars, if possible)
- ink pad

*H*appiness is

not a station you

arrive at, but a

manner of

traveling.

— Margaret Lee Runbeck
Author (1905-1956)

PROCEDURE:

At the beginning of the year or unit, have students reflect on the quality of their own character. Distribute the self-assessment and have students rate on a scale of 1-10 how much they agree with each statement, then add up their points to get an overall score. (You could also conduct a formal survey to get a baseline assessment of students.)

Issue a character passport to students. Tell them, *In order to travel around the world, you must have a passport. It is a little booklet that has your picture, name and address, and authorizes you to enter other countries. When you go to a different country, an official stamps your passport to document your arrival and departure. I am going to give you a character passport. It will authorize you to go on a journey of character development, to learn about the Six Pillars of Character.* As lessons on each Pillar are completed, stamp each student's passport in the corresponding box. Alternately, give the stamp only when students demonstrate the Pillar being studied. At the end of the year or unit, have students reassess themselves to see how much they've improved (or the teacher can give a follow-up survey).

read up and reach out at www.charactercounts.org

Character Self-Assessment

Rate how much you agree with each statement below on a scale of 1-10. A score of 1 means you do not agree at all with the statement, and 10 means you agree completely. This exercise is intended to help you see your current strengths and weaknesses, so please be honest.

_____ I tell the truth all the time.

_____ I am a loyal friend.

_____ When I say I'm going to do something, I follow through.

_____ I treat others the way I want them to treat me.

_____ I say *please* and *thank you*, and otherwise show good manners.

_____ I treat all people, even those who are different from me, with respect.

_____ I do not tease, insult or bully people.

_____ I always do my best.

_____ My parents only have to tell me to do something once, and I do it.

_____ I never lose my temper.

_____ I practice good listening skills in conversations.

_____ I am tolerant of other people's opinions.

_____ I am compassionate toward those who have less than I do.

_____ I give compliments to people.

_____ I like to do nice things for people.

_____ I always do my share of the chores at home.

_____ When I play games, I always follow the rules.

_____ I obey the law.

_____ **TOTAL**

Self-Assessment Scoring Guide

150-180: You have a strong character and should be proud of yourself. Learning the Six Pillars will help you be an even better person!

120-149: You do the right thing more often than not, but could use some improvement in making the best choice in challenging situations.

90-119: You really need to work on improving your character, and the Six Pillars will help you do that!

Below 90: Good for you that you were at least honest in filling out this assessment. As you commit to developing the Six Pillars within yourself, you will notice a big change for the better in your character.

read up and reach out at www.charactercounts.org

The Six Pillars of Character are T.R.R.F.C.C.

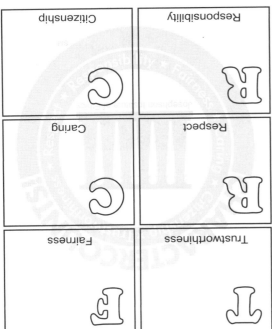

Responsibility	Citizenship
R	C
Respect	Caring
R	C
Trustworthiness	Fairness
T	F

Signature

Purpose of Visit

City / Country of Origin

Name (please print)

Place photo or drawing of yourself here.

CHARACTERCOUNTS!sm

The Six Pillars of Character

Trustworthiness Be honest • Don't deceive, cheat or steal • Be reliable — do what you say you'll do • Have the courage to do the right thing • Build a good reputation • Be loyal — stand by your family, friends and country

Respect Treat others with respect; follow the Golden Rule • Be tolerant of differences • Use good manners, not bad language • Be considerate of the feelings of others • Don't threaten, hit or hurt anyone • Deal peacefully with anger, insults and disagreements

Responsibility Do what you are supposed to do • Persevere: keep on trying! • Always do your best • Use self-control • Be self-disciplined • Think before you act — consider the consequences • Be accountable for your choices

Fairness Play by the rules • Take turns and share • Be open-minded; listen to others • Don't take advantage of others • Don't blame others carelessly

Caring Be kind • Be compassionate and *show* you care • Express gratitude • Forgive others • Help people in need

Citizenship Do your share to make your school and community better • Cooperate • Stay informed; vote • Be a good neighbor • Obey laws and rules • Respect authority • Protect the environment

charactercounts.org

CHARACTERCOUNTS!sm
SIX PILLAR
Passport

Your CHARACTER COUNTS! Everywhere ... All the Time!

More Good Ideas to Help Young People Develop Good Character

CHARACTER DEVELOPMENT SEMINARS

is the country's leading training program for character-education specialists. This three-day course provides practical strategies and materials and certifies participants to prepare others to be effective character educators. Also available: community awareness seminars, customized in-service training and advanced training for graduates — as well as training seminars on building character through sports and in the workplace.

PURSUING VICTORY WITH HONOR (PVWH)

is a sportsmanship campaign endorsed by virtually every major American amateur athletic group, from the NCAA Division I and the National Basketball Coaches Association to the Big Ten Conference and the U.S. Olympic Committee, Coaches Division. Services and materials include Ethics in Sports seminars, the PVWH Ultimate Sportsmanship Tool Kit, customized vinyl banners and more. For entertaining stories and useful tips, subscribe to the free monthly PVWH e-newsletter (see www.charactercounts.org/newsletters.htm).

For more information about these services and support materials, please call us at (800) 711-2670 or visit us online at CHARACTERCOUNTS.ORG.

You can also go online to receive scores of free resources such as handouts, newsletters, essays and sample lesson plans — as well as order any of our vast range of creative, professionally designed, age-appropriate support materials, including books, booklets, videos, music, posters, banners and more. We are dedicated to serving you. Please let us know how we can.

USEFUL REPORTS

published by the Josephson Institute of Ethics include *The Report Card on the Ethics of American Youth 2004* (available Oct. '04), *Gold Medal Standards for Youth Sports, The Hidden Costs of Unethical Behavior, Youth and Violence: What We Can Do About It,* and more.

HONOR ABOVE ALL

is a new integrity promotion campaign that provides teachers with resources to prevent cheating and create a climate of honesty.